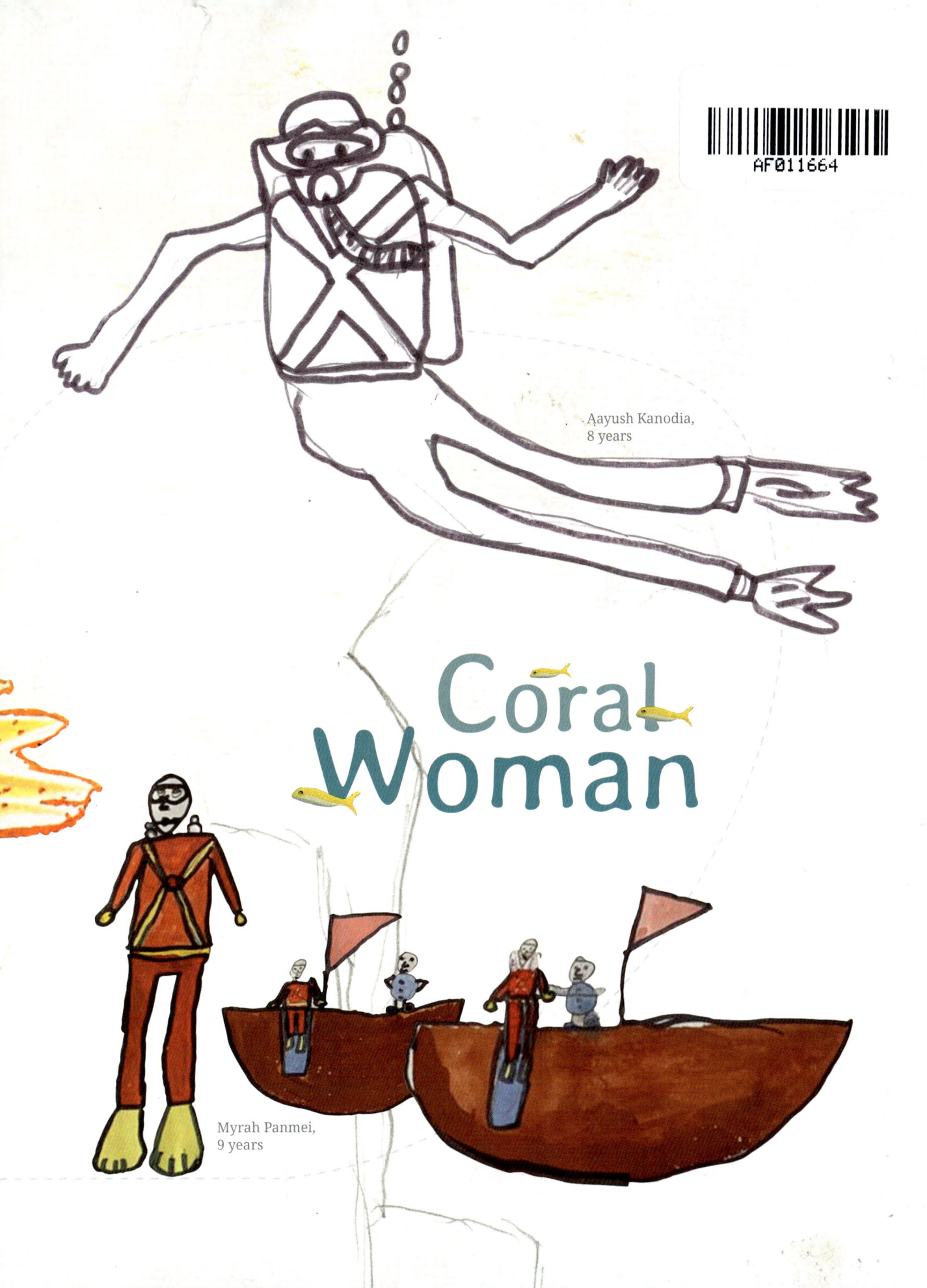

First published in India in 2021 by HarperCollins Children's Books
An imprint of HarperCollins Publishers
A-75, Sector 57, Noida, Uttar Pradesh 201301, India
www.harpercollins.co.in

2 4 6 8 10 9 7 5 3 1
Text ©Avid Learning and T&M Productions 2021
Illustrations ©Avid Learning and T&M Productions 2021

P-ISBN: 978-93-5489-300-1
E-ISBN: 978-93-5489-302-5

Lubaina Bandukwala and Sanket Pethkar assert the moral right
to be identified as the author and illustrator of this work.

All rights reserved. No part of this publication may be reproduced,
stored in a retrieval system, or transmitted, in any form or by any means,
electronic, mechanical, photocopying, recording or otherwise,
without the prior permission of the publishers.

Book design and layout: Ketul Patel
@limmer13

Artwork photography: Sandeep Savant
@savant505

Typeset in Droid Serif 11pt/18

Printed and bound at Thomson Press India Ltd

Coral Woman

Dive into the Majestic World of
Coral Reefs with Uma Mani!

Based on *CORAL WOMAN*, a film by **Priya Thuvassery**

Written by **Lubaina Bandukwala**
Illustrated by **Sanket Pethkar**

Book conceptualised
and supported by

Contents

Prologue 06

Chapter 1
The Goddess from Under the Sea... 10
What are corals? 11

Chapter 2
New is Scary! 14

Chapter 3
Catch the Tiger by the Tail 18

Chapter 4
Dive! 22
Nature's paintbox 25
The coral reef is a wonderland of life 25

Chapter 5

An Underwater Graveyard 28
Coral reefs of India 30

Chapter 6

Coral plus Pollution – Bad Idea! 34
Bleaching? What is that? 35

Chapter 7

Planting an Underwater Garden 38
How to grow a coral 41

Prologue

"Jump!"
It was the moment she had been waiting for. And yet,
when the time came, she just couldn't do it.
"Jump!"
"No."
"Jump!" he repeated.
"No," she replied, suddenly afraid.
Until a few months ago, 45-year-old Uma Mani hadn't even known how to swim. Yet now she had set out to dive into the deep sea.
Then suddenly the dive master gave her a nudge and she flipped backwards from the boat into the deep dark waters.

The cool water embraced her like a mother, and gentle currents rocked her as if the sea was singing a lullaby. She swam to the sea floor to see for herself what she had dreamed of for years – the brilliant colours and fantastic shapes of a coral reef.

Swimming over the reef, she marvelled at the table coral – bigger than a dining table, with edges that looked exactly like white lace. She exclaimed at one that even looked like a biryani pot. And the fishes! She found herself in the middle of a school of fish that was almost 1.5 kilometres long! "I couldn't even see the water," she said with wonder.

And from the moment she stepped into their underwater realm she became a life-long crusader of coral reefs.

A crusade that wasn't as simple as it seems.

1
The Goddess from Under the Sea

Uma was in her 40s. She lived with her husband and son in the Maldives where her husband, a doctor, had an assignment. Like many homemakers, most of her days were centred around the routine of home and family. But Uma had one defining characteristic. Curiosity. "I want to keep learning something new all the time!" she laughed. In this case it was – no, not diving, but French!

One day, the French class had to attend a special event. They were to watch a film about coral reefs. Uma, always enthusiastic about anything new, came to watch. She wasn't really expecting to find it interesting, yet from the very first shot, she was hooked! She was entranced by the corals, the underwater creatures and most of all by a woman coral researcher in the movie. The researcher in the film was dressed in a diving suit and to Uma she looked like some sort of superhero, and the underwater world like some sort of magical kingdom. "I was awed! I wanted to be just like her – wear a diving suit and swim the oceans," she laughed.

That said, at that point the possibility of Uma learning to dive seemed far away. Uma had never learned how to swim. In fact she would barely go ankle deep in beautiful seas off the Maldives. But unwittingly, a seed was sown. She was thoroughly intrigued by the world under the sea, especially corals and this was to take her down a most adventurous path.

With that film, the pull of the ocean had cast its spell. Since she never thought that she could ever see the corals herself, she decided to do the next best thing. With her husband's help she collected a whole lot of pictures and videos of corals. Then, armed with paints, brushes and canvas, Uma began to paint the beauty of the world she longed to see.

Soumil Rathi, 12 years

What are corals?

The word coral comes from the scientific name of the Mediterranean red coral Coralliym rubrum which was celebrated for its beautiful red colour. Corals are animals or tiny creatures called polyps that live underwater. Each soft-bodied polyp secretes a hard outer skeleton of limestone (calcium carbonate) that attaches either to rock or the dead skeletons of other polyps. These polyps grow, die, and endlessly repeat the cycle over time, slowly laying the limestone foundation for coral reefs.

There are as many as 5080 species of corals all over the world. Corals can live for hundreds of years. A deep water coral reef off the coast of Hawaii is more than 4000 years old.

It took as much as 20,000 years to build the 3,48,000 square kilometres of the Great Barrier Reef off the coast of Australia – the largest reef on Earth.

2
New is Scary!

When you find a passion – wonderful things happen. For one, you grow as you learn more about your new-found passion. "I became so fascinated by corals," says Uma. "I tried to learn everything I could from wherever I could. And actually I was in the right place for it."

The Maldives is an island nation with 26 atolls surrounded by coral reefs. It plays host to numerous conferences and coral conservation projects. Uma used every opportunity to speak with conference attendees and local conservationists.

For the first time in all the years they had lived in the Maldives, Uma also became more aware of the world around her. "The Maldives has the most beautiful sandy beaches, and just a little further from the shore you can see so many corals, but I just didn't notice them!"

And most of all, she found the courage to step out of her comfort zone and try something new.

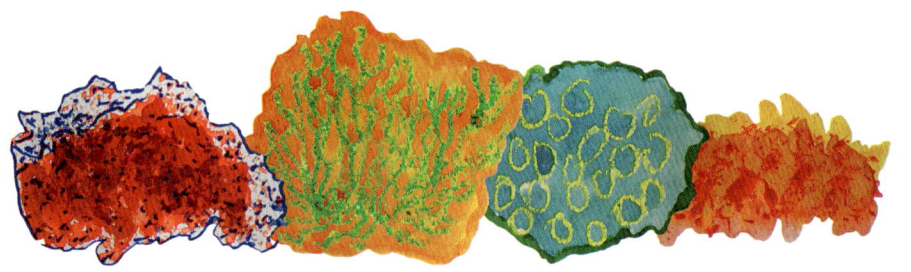

Akaisha Mahadevan Krishnamoorthy,
10 years

The gorgeous Maldives islands are dotted with hotels that often run marine centres as tourist attractions. Uma secured an invitation to exhibit her paintings at one such hotel on World Environment Day. Of course, since she hadn't done anything like this before she was hesitant, but she also wanted to share her paintings with a wider audience. And so, she decided that the experience would be worth it.

And what an experience it turned out to be! "The hotel sent a fancy motorboat for me and I put all my canvases in it and went there. There were so many firsts on this trip," she remembers. First she had never exhibited her paintings before so she had to put them up single-handedly and get them ready for an exhibition. Then she had to chat with people from around the world who were at the hotel. And most of all, she had to deal with the challenge of spending the night away from home alone.

As part of the offer, the hotel put her up in one of their luxury suites – one of their most expensive. And yet for Uma it held no attraction. Uma had never spent a night away from her husband and son. So having this whole room to herself was unnerving! "I had never stayed away from my family" she laughs. "I was so scared to sleep by myself that I didn't sleep a wink!"

Uma sold only one painting at the exhibition, but the trip was valuable in many other ways. She now felt so much more confident and was thrilled to learn more from the young divers in the conservation centre who had dived in sites around the world!

Also as a result other hotels too began to exhibit her work. And it was at one such exhibition that an event occurred that was to change her life.

3
Catch the Tiger by the Tail

It was 2014, she remembers, the year she was exhibiting at the Taj in the Maldives. Uma was at the exhibition of her paintings when a couple from Delhi walked in. Ever friendly, Uma went forward to chat with the lady, but she turned out to be quite snobbish and not interested in speaking with her. She glanced around the exhibition and told Uma, "Have you ever seen the reef yourself?"

"No," Uma replied. "I think you should," she said dismissively, and walked away.

That hurt! In the short time that Uma had started going out hesitantly to exhibit paintings of her beloved corals, most visitors responded to her friendliness with warmth. She had

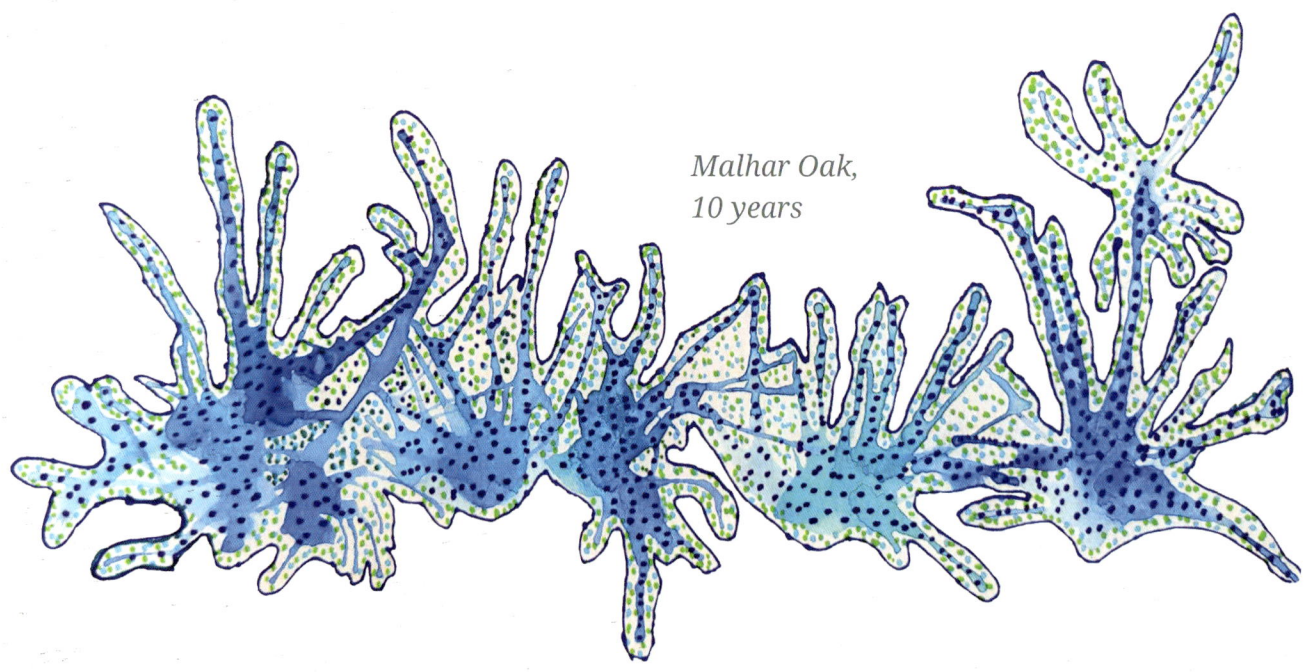

*Malhar Oak,
10 years*

never met with harsh criticism. She had never encountered this kind of rudeness! The lady's words and attitude really jolted her – and to have someone dismiss her work and her passion made Uma really sad and disheartened.

However, Uma felt that there was something to be learnt here. She remembers thinking, "People close to me, they wouldn't tell me the truth because they don't want to hurt me. But this lady, she is right, something in my paintings is missing because I haven't seen the corals myself," Uma recalls. Uma realised that despite what she had learnt about corals from others, her understanding was limited since she had not seen the corals firsthand!

And from that moment on, Uma was determined to find a way to visit the coral reefs herself. "Can I learn to dive?" she wondered. It was a daunting task. "I had a lot of fears. Most people considered it strange that at this stage of my life, I wanted to do something so adventurous. I myself was a bit scared of water – but as we say in Tamil Pulivalaalai pidithathu pola, I decided to catch the tiger by the tail instead of running away like I wanted to."

It so happened that she had to go to Chennai for two months that year. In those two months, since she was staying with family she was free of household responsibilities. "It's now or never," she thought, "I'll never get this chance again." So she put aside all her anxiety and embarrassment and learnt how to swim. Of course, she still had no idea how she would learn to dive, but the first step had been taken. And as we well know, fortune favours the brave and a surprise awaited her on her return.

4
Dive!

*Shrey Warrier,
12 years*

That year Uma and her husband were celebrating their 25th wedding anniversary. And even as Uma was wondering how to save up for the expense of diving lessons, her son gave her a unique anniversary present – a diving course! What's more, it was a diving course in one of the most beautiful diving locations in the world – the Maldives. "I had a friend, Shahina Ma'am – she was very encouraging. She said, 'Uma I know you can learn how to dive'. And when I was able to take the course I went to her husband's diving school. Let me tell you, as enthusiastic as I was, this was the hardest thing I had ever done!"

When you learn diving, a lot of the lessons take place on land, long before you actually go under the sea. "I had to learn how to wear the gear and it was so heavy!" In fact she was so intimidated that for almost a month she pretended she had a cold so she couldn't go to class (you are not allowed to dive when you have a cold). "Throughout that time I kept giving myself pep talks. I told myself, I've got to do this. This is a chance of a lifetime! And my son, he spent so much money on such a special gift!" she smiles, reminiscing fondly.

One day, she once again caught the tiger by the tail and went back to continue her course. However, when she went out on the boat to the open seas, her courage failed her, and her dive master had to push her in. That one push gave her a ringside seat in one of nature's most spectacular theatres – The Coral Reef.

The reef underwater was everything Uma imagined it to be. After that day she was to go on six dives and each one would be unique. In the timelessness of the clear blue waters she saw fields and fields of sea anemones swaying gently, with hundreds of fish and electric eels slipping through the corals.

She swam identifying all the corals that she had painted but never really seen. "The shapes, the forms, the colours were so beautiful. The leather coral is my favourite – it looks as if these are folds of leather sitting on the sea floor," she marvelled.

One day, almost at the end of the dive when they were getting ready to go back up to the surface, her diving instructor pointed above her. Looking up she saw a huge majestic sea turtle gently making its way through the water. "We followed it for a while, slowly gliding through the reef, it was just beautiful."

"Heading back in an open van to the dive centre always gave me a great sense of freedom. I was tired and very hungry. I would eat and go off to sleep. But my head, it was still under the water – I could think of nothing else except the images, the life, the movement and the stillness of the coral reef."

"When I was a child, I loved to tell stories. When I would watch a movie and come back, all my cousins and friends would gather around me to hear the story. At school too in the free period, I would go up and tell stories. If I saw something beautiful I would have to share that with everyone," says Uma.

So when she saw the reefs and learnt more about them she wanted to tell the whole world about them.

Finally, Uma gathered the courage to ring up NDTV. Of course at first no one took her seriously. But soon she crossed paths with Senior Producer Priya Thuvassery. At that time Priya was unable to cover that story. However, some years later, when she became an independent filmmaker, she remembered the phone call from the shy yet determined woman and thus was born the film, *Coral Woman*. And also a whole new adventure.

Meysha Correa,
9 years

Nature's paintbox

Uma's desire to paint the corals is understandable. Who wouldn't want to capture the incredible colours and shapes of a coral reef? Do you know where corals get their colour from?

Living within the cells of corals are tiny algae called Zooxanthellae. Zooxanthellae manufacture food by photosynthesis and provide corals with energy. In return, the corals provide the algae with a home and the basic compounds they need for photosynthesis. Zooxanthellae give their hosts one more gift – the myriad colours that are found in corals.

Coral reef is a wonderland of life

Coral reefs occupy less than 0.1% of the world's ocean area, about half the area of France, yet they provide a home for at least 25% of all marine species.

Corals grow in hundreds of beautiful shapes. The carnation coral has pearly white stems with carnation flower-shaped heads in vibrant colours. The Venus sea fan is like a delicate lace fan and the sun coral comes in shades of yellow, orange, red and pink.

Some amazing creatures live here. The giant clam can grow up to four feet and can weigh more than 200 kg! The parrot fish makes itself a small sack of saliva to sleep in at night to protect it from predators.

5
An Underwater Graveyard

Uma was now an experienced diver. But she had never seen the coral reefs along India's coasts. So she set off to explore these with Priya. Her first port of call was Thoothukudi (formerly Tuticorin) in Tamil Nadu. Thoothukudi is a coastal town. It is one tip of an arc that ends at Rameswaram along the Gulf of Mannar. In these waters lies the Mannar Barrier Reef one of four coral reefs in Indian waters.

Thoothukudi was famous in history. So famous, that even the Romans knew about it 3000 years ago! Off the coast of this city were tall reefs, more than 10 feet high, rich with pearl oysters. Divers all along the coast dived into these waters and plucked out pearl oysters making Tuticorin a renowned trading centre for pearls.

It was here that Uma made her first dive into Indian waters. And she was stunned. This time, not by the beauty of

Anaiya Rathi,
10 years

the reef, but by the desolation. "Where were the glorious corals that divers plucked pearl oysters from? What happened to the colours? What happened to the fish that should have been darting around in this, their home? This is a coral graveyard!" she thought.

One by one the questions came up underwater. But the answers lay above it.

Some answers she found on a walk – a walk that took her around the city looking closely at walls of homes. Walls that were built not of brick, or of cement, but of coral. Until 2005 large amounts of coral were mined from the reef for various reasons, including as building material for homes.

Some answers she found with a swim – a swim of a different kind. One morning she set off on a boat with a few local divers. Men and women. The latter, sari-clad with goggles, gloves and flippers who dived into the waters with net bags. Were they looking for pearls? No. Not pearls. Nestled among the withering corals were vistas of algae – Kappaphycus alvarezii. The fisherfolk swam around collecting these and filling their baskets. "What are these?" Uma asked. These algae, native to the Philippines were brought and replanted by authorities to create livelihoods, she was told. This algae is the source of a substance called carrageenan, which is used widely in various products including a top soft drink brand and toothpaste. Harvesting this algae is easy money since companies pay a lot of money for this. Unfortunately, the algae is not a native species and thus has no check. It is growing so fast, it is overtaking the coral.

Other answers she found during chats with folks in the region. They took her to drains and nallas that discharge untreated sewage into the sea, making it polluted. At the other end of the Gulf, at Rameswaram, she was horrified to see piles of clothes discarded on the beach by bathing pilgrims and tourists as well as sewage from the hotels close by. And then there was damage from the massive thermal plant that spews hot water into the sea. This plant also belches so much fly ash, that a portion of the sea has become concrete!

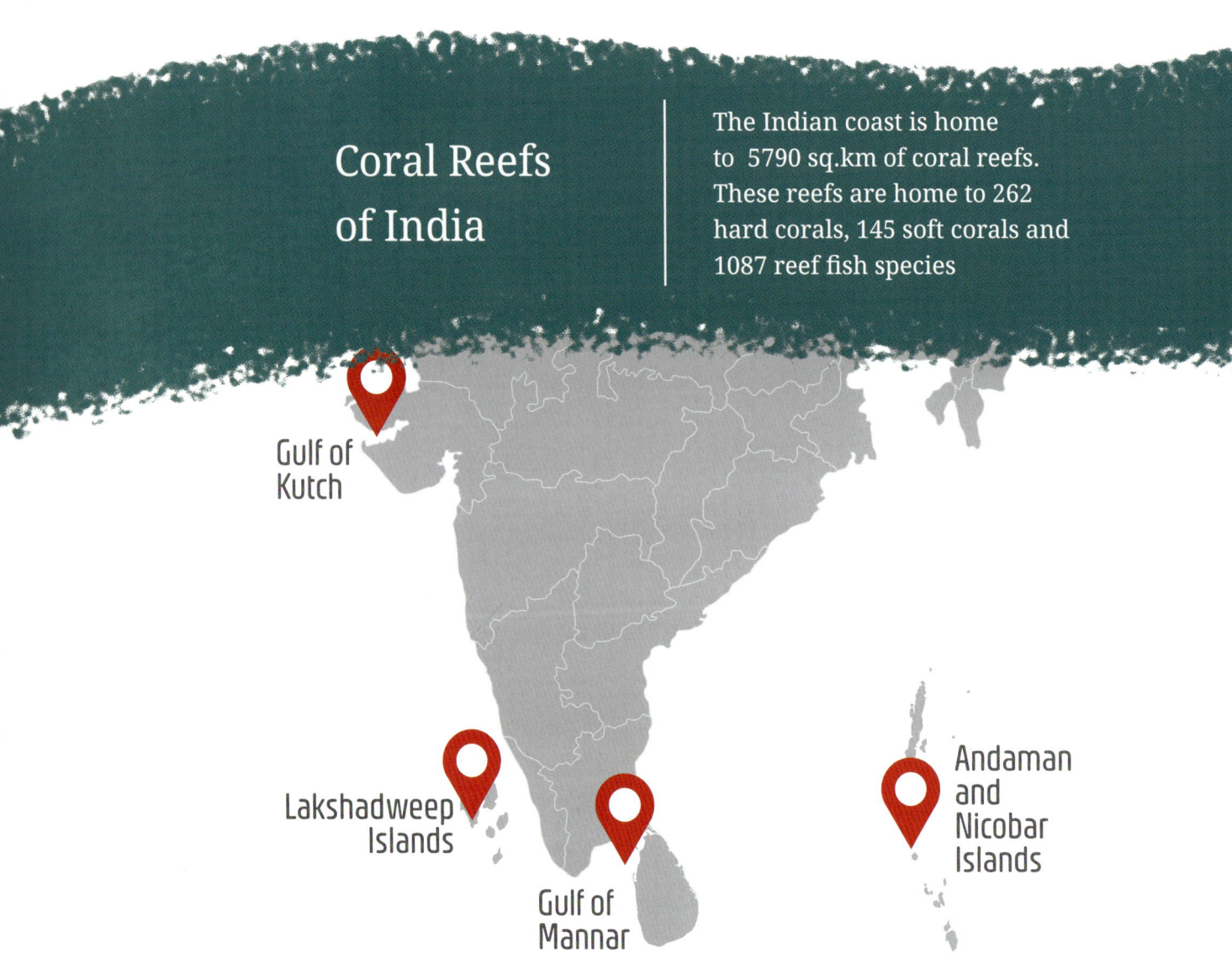

Coral Reefs of India

The Indian coast is home to 5790 sq.km of coral reefs. These reefs are home to 262 hard corals, 145 soft corals and 1087 reef fish species

- Gulf of Kutch
- Lakshadweep Islands
- Gulf of Mannar
- Andaman and Nicobar Islands

📍 Lakshadweep islands
Six islands, 12 atolls, 3 reefs, 5 submerged banks with 134 species of corals. In 2020, the world's first sea cucumber conservation area was established here – The Dr. K. K. Mohammed Koya Sea Cucumber Reserve. A profusion of the blue coral species is the speciality here.

📍 Gulf of Kutch
The area is characterised by patchy reefs growing on sandstone platforms and has 42 species of hard corals and 10 soft coral ones. The reefs are threatened by high salinity, temperature fluctuations and heavy sedimentation. A marine national park has been established here for conservation.

📍 Gulf of Mannar
Twenty-one islands comprise the reef area. The reef flat region is extensive here. Marine debris, pollution and fishing are the major threats. Coral mining during the previous decades was another cause of concern in this region. A biodiversity reserve was established here to ensure conservation.

📍 Andaman and Nicobar Islands
These coral reefs are ecologically more similar to the reefs in other Southeast Asian seas. This is because of the ocean currents that cause the exchange of larva. The reefs show a high degree of diversity. Minor reefs include the Gaveshani Bank, 100 km offshore Mangalore, the Malvan reef, a reef sanctuary in Mumbai and occasional coral patches on the West Coast.

Source: Coral Woman Impact Project, T&M Productions

6
Coral plus Pollution – Bad Idea!

Pollution causes acidification which can limit coral growth. It can damage coral skeletons and also slow the growth of new ones. The weaker reefs that are formed as a result will be more vulnerable to erosion.

Coral reefs were already affected by mining and pollution, but the biggest blow came from sources no one could control locally – global warming. In 2016, there occurred an event that ecologists call the second global bleaching event in which sea temperatures rose bleaching reefs around the world including those in the Gulf of Mannar. As many as 16.2 percent of corals in this area were lost then.

Okay, so this damaged eroded reef lies underwater, out of sight from our world. Why should that matter to us?

That's because Coral is Nature's Thermometer.

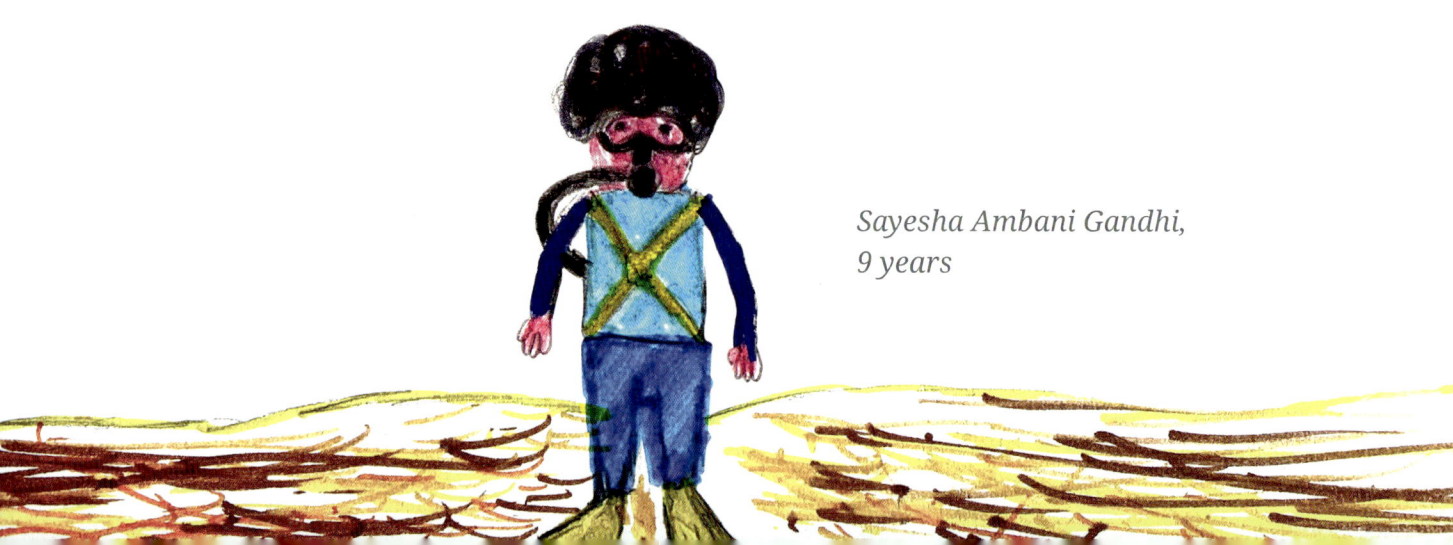

Sayesha Ambani Gandhi, 9 years

Here is something you should know about corals. They tell you about the health of the sea, like a thermometer that checks if you have a fever. Is the water clean? Unpolluted? The right temperature? Is it too salty? If all is well, corals will thrive. And when they thrive, they offer the promise of life to hundreds of creatures that shelter in their nooks and crannies. "The coral needs fish and fish need coral – that is the truth I learnt," says Uma when she found out that so many species of fish are disappearing along the coast of Mannar.

The corals also protect the coast and small islands from tidal waves and erosion. How important is this? You'll soon find out.

Bleaching? What is that?

The coral's hard external skeleton is occupied by organisms called zooxanthellae, which give the coral colour. They live in the coral and in return produce food by photosynthesis that they share with the coral. When the water gets too hot (or too cold) or gets extra salty or acidic (because of pollutants) the zooxanthellae exit the coral leaving the coral white or bleached. This coral will die in a bit, since without the zooxanthellae it will not have any food!

7
Planting an Underwater Garden

Uma now lives far away from the sea. She lives in the hills and lovingly farms her land. She continues to paint her coral canvases. Often you will find her painting the intricate patterns, the unique qualities and the brilliant colours of the corals. But now she also paints in sombre elements – the blues of plastic that floats in from the mountain streams into the sea. The thermal plant in fiery red and stark black looming over the fragile coral ecosystem.

Naisha Kanodia,
10 years

"The more I saw the corals and the beauty of the sea, the more mindful I became of the world around me. I realised that everything we do affects something somewhere in the world." Hence, although she lives in the mountains, she realised that everything there eventually affects the oceans. If you pollute the mountain streams, the pollutants will flow down to the sea. If you cut the forests, the atmosphere warms up and the coral gets bleached. Hundreds of things we do, affect hundreds of people hundreds of miles away from us. So in her daily life too she is more mindful. Her family has adopted solar power in their home. She only uses cloth shopping bags. These are small lifestyle changes that she believes will make a big difference.

Everywhere she goes, she shows her paintings and her underwater videos. She shares them with school children and governments. With local communities and far off ones. She urges them to protect the corals, to save them, for their own livelihoods depend on them.

But she also dreams of growing corals. Is that possible? In order to answer that question, Uma took yet another fascinating journey. Near Tuticorin is the Gulf of Mannar Marine National Park. This is composed of 21 islands and the reefs that surround them. That is, there were once 21 islands. Now two of them are under the sea, since the surrounding reefs that protected them from the tidal waves and erosion are gone. And one more, Vaan Island is sinking so quickly that it seems in the next 30 years it will also be gone.

Maybe not.

Marine biologists at Vaan Island are conducting an experiment to replant and grow corals that were native to the area around the island. If successful, it could be the formula to help damaged reefs recover. Can that happen? Maybe. Time will tell. And this is the hope, the desire to replant the grand underwater forests full of myriad creatures.

From one glimpse of the reefs in a film seen many years ago to actively educating people about reefs and working to conserve their habitat, Uma has come a long way. Besides having solar panels on her roof and using cloth bags for shopping, she now uses public transport for travel and even does rainwater harvesting.

She has made it her life's work to nurture the coral reefs and to protect an ecosystem that keeps our coasts healthy and rich. "Let me share my world with you," she says, drawing us deep into the magical underwater forests that are the coral reefs. "It is more beautiful than you can imagine."

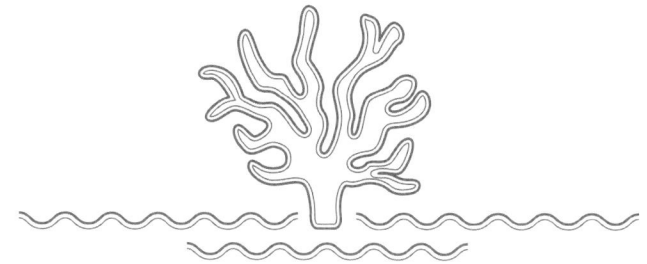

How to grow a coral?

Corals can propagate both asexually and sexually. Both these methods can be used to grow coral. In the former, bits of live coral broken off from reefs can be tied to a substrate (like broken pieces of coral skeleton etc.) and placed on the sea floor. In due course, the coral will grow attaching itself to the old skeleton. This is how it is done in coral conservation projects in Thoothukudi, Tamil Nadu.

In the latter, the male and female gametes are fused and put on a substrate and placed on the seafloor, as shown below.

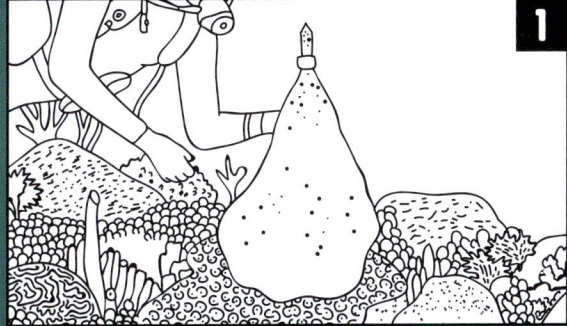

During the natural cycle of reproduction on a reef, corals produce male and female gametes which then release eggs and sperms over a large area. These are collected by conservationists.

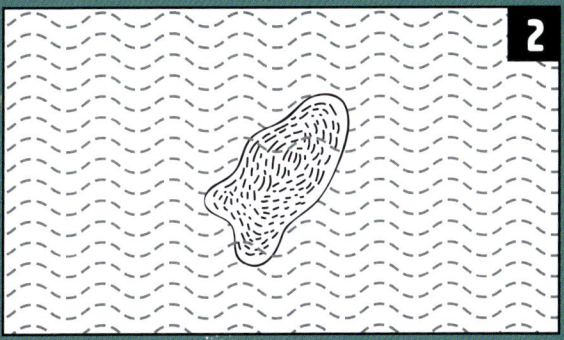

The eggs and sperm fuse to form larvae called planulae.

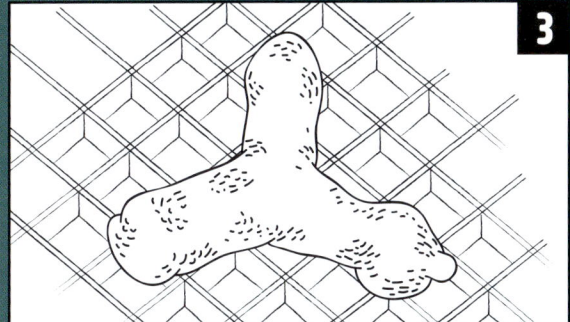

The larvae are placed on a base like cement pods or dead coral, where each one settles and changes into a polyp no larger than a millimetre.

Each larva begins to clone and form colonies of corals made up of many tiny polyps. These are placed on the sea floor to form a coral reef.

A special thank you to **Smiti Kanodia** without whose support this book would not have been possible. **Asad Lalljee** *& the Avid Learning Team and* **Sophy Sivaraman** *& the Good Pitch India Team.*

The book also features illustrations created by children between the ages of 9-14 years who participated in Coral Woman, A Sketching and Book Illustration Workshop facilitated by children's illustrator **Zainab Tambawalla**. The workshop was conceptualised and presented by *Avid Learning*.

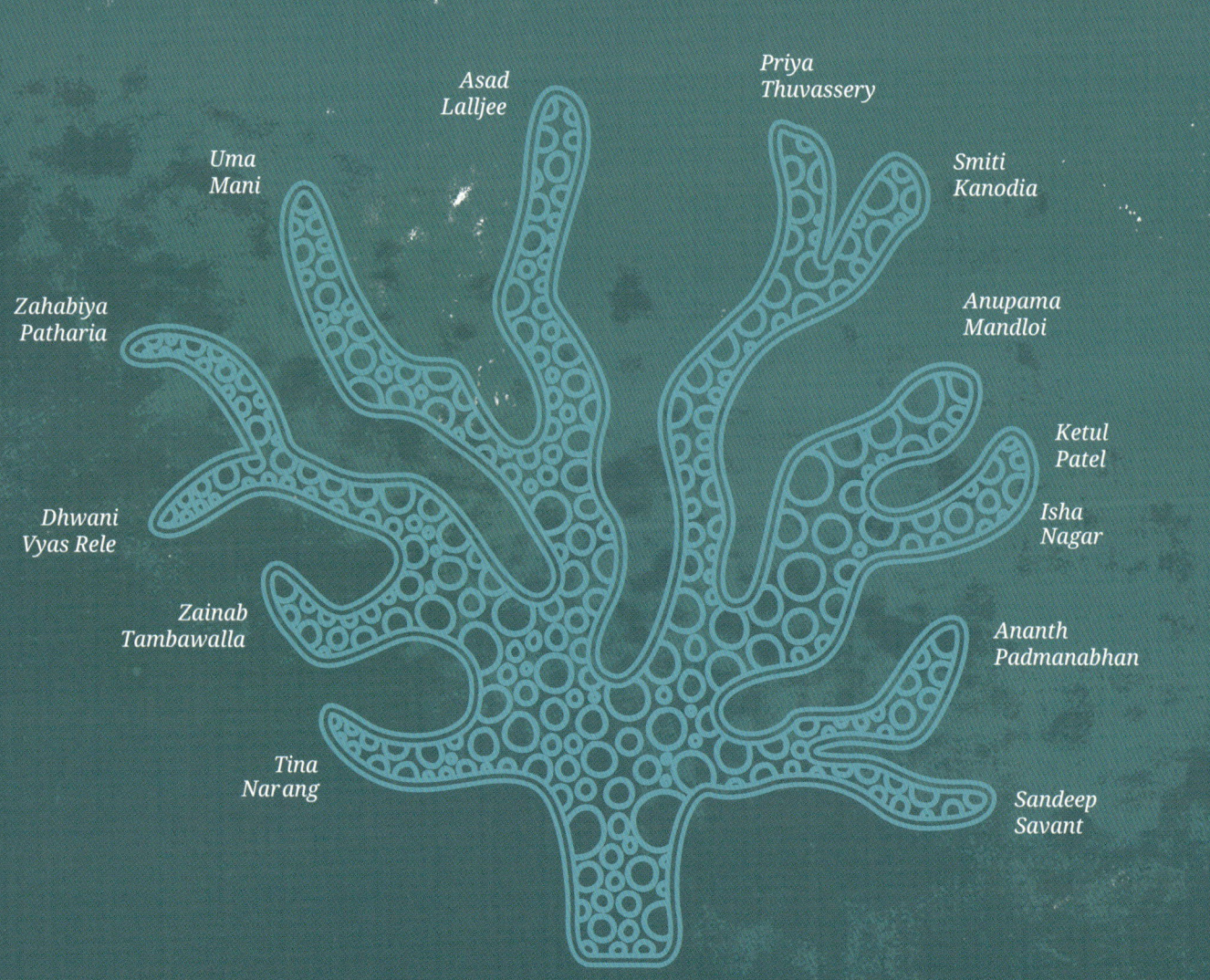

Asad Lalljee
Priya Thuvassery
Uma Mani
Smiti Kanodia
Zahabiya Patharia
Anupama Mandloi
Ketul Patel
Dhwani Vyas Rele
Isha Nagar
Zainab Tambawalla
Ananth Padmanabhan
Tina Narang
Sandeep Savant

About the creators

Lubaina Bandukwala is a writer and editor of children's books and founder of Peek A Book Literature Festival for kids.

Sanket Pethkar is a picture book artist based in Mumbai. He has been the recipient of Jarul Picture Book Award in 2017, for *The Night Monster* by Sushree Mishra and published by Karadi Tales.

Priya Thuvassery is an independent documentary filmmaker and television producer for over a decade now. She is currently an Executive Producer at Chambal Media and is leading the impact project for her latest film *Coral Woman*.

Asad Lalljee is a Cultural Catalyst, Curator & Producer, former New Yorker & advertising Mad Man, CEO Avid Learning, Curator of Royal Opera House, Mumbai and a believer in #LearningNeverStops

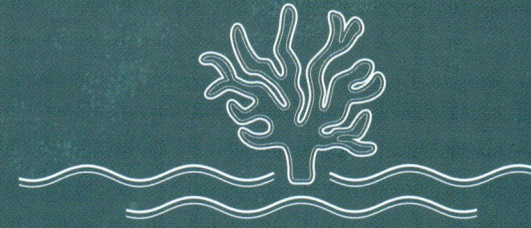

For more information about the film, about coral reefs and to buy Uma's paintings visit https://coralwoman.com

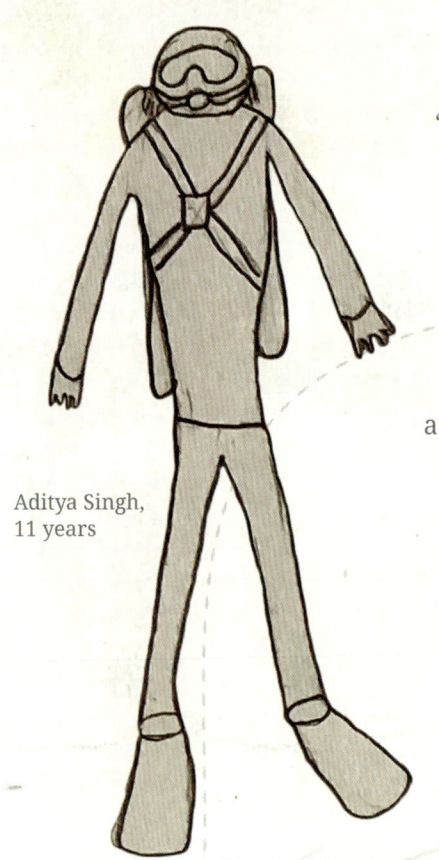

Aditya Singh,
11 years

"One passionate woman can change the world. That reality is what Uma Mani - Coral Woman - puts exquisitely into play, with help from the celebratory vision of children... whose elders thoughtlessly dismantle their only home.

We came from the sea and will return to the sea. In the interim Uma Mani poignantly asks that we marvel - and protect - its treasures."

BITTU SAHGAL
Editor, Sanctuary Asia

Zahra Faizullabhoy,
12 years

"There is so much to love about Coral Woman. Not just her passion for underwater life and understanding the environment, but her bravery and curiosity that pushes her to keep pushing herself. We need more role models like Uma Mani!"

DIVIA THANI
Global Editorial Director,
Conde Nast Traveller

"Coral Woman is an evocative, heartwarming story that inspires genuine wonder for coral reefs! At a time when our oceans and coral reefs are confronting grave environmental challenges, the next generation needs more stories of our personal connection to the natural world, and that's what this book does exceptionally!"

MALAIKA VAZ
Filmmaker and Founder, Untamed Planet

Zambian Wadhwani,
10 years